THE UNTOLD STORY OF
EL HADJ SAAD OUMAR TOURE
A Visionary Who Transformed Islamic Education in West Africa

BabouConnect Publishing

Copyright © [2025] Mahamadou Saad Toure
All rights reserved.

No part of this book may be reproduced, stored in a retrieval system, or transmitted in any form or by any means—electronic, mechanical, photocopying, recording, or otherwise—without the prior written permission of the publisher, except in the case of brief quotations embodied in critical reviews and certain other noncommercial uses as permitted by copyright law.

Published by : BabouConnect Publishing

ISBN: [979-8-9939072-6-0]

["Printed in [USA]"]
Interior layout & cover by [Mahamadou S. Toure]

For permissions, inquiries, or bulk orders, contact:
[sabilfalah@gmail.com]

This is a work of nonfiction. The events and figures depicted are based on historical facts, author research, and firsthand accounts. Any errors or omissions are unintentional.

First Edition: [2025]

To the memory of my father, El Hadj Saad Oumar Toure
A visionary, an educator, and a pillar of faith.
Your legacy continues to inspire generations.
To my son, Saad
May you always carry the light of knowledge and faith forward.

Contents

Preface..vii

Introduction..1

Chapter-1: Early Life and Background...............5
   Early Childhood & Family Influence......................5

Chapter-2: Education & Overcoming Challenges......11
   Forced into the French Colonial School System.............12
   Balancing French Education with Islamic Studies..........13
   A Turning Point: A Merchant with a Mission................16

Chapter-3 : The Birth of a Dream: Establishing **Medersah Sébil El Falah**..21
   A Humble Beginning: The First Classroom............22
   Resistance from the Community.............................23
   The Colonial Government's Attempt to Buy Him Out......26

Chapter-4 : Saad's Personal Contributions: His Books, **Innovations, and Growing Influence**........................33
   The Scholar & Author: Writing for the Next Generation.....35
   A Scholar and a Global Explorer..............................38
   A Legacy in Motion..43

Chapter-5 : **A Leader Beyond the Classroom: Personal Leadership, Family, and Final Years**..............................45

    Compassion for Students: No Child Left Behind................47

    A Mentor Beyond His Household............................48

    Strict but Fair Leadership....................................48

Chapter-6 : **Personal Experience**............................51

    As a Student...51

    The Contrast Between Father and Son's Experience............53

    Final Years: A Life Dedicated Until the Last Breath.............55

Chapter-7 : **The Living Legacy of El Hadj Saad Oumar Toure: A Legacy That Transcends Time**........................59

Author's Note..61

Personal Reflection: A Son's Tribute...................63

Preface

This book is more than just a biography, it is a tribute to a man whose vision transformed lives. **El Hadj Saad Oumar Toure** was not only my father but also a pioneer, an educator, and a guardian of knowledge. His unwavering faith, resilience, and dedication to Islamic education shaped generations, leaving a legacy that continues to inspire.

Growing up, I witnessed firsthand the impact of his teachings. His school, **Medersah Sébil El Falah**, was more than a place of learning, it was a beacon of hope, a foundation for those seeking both spiritual and intellectual growth. His leadership, his sacrifices, and his commitment to building a better future were lessons not just taught in words, but lived through his actions.

This book is the **untold story** of a man who **defied colonial pressures, resisted cultural erosion, and revolutionized Islamic education** in West Africa. It is also a deeply personal journey for me, as I recount the wisdom, struggles, and triumphs of my father, his quiet moments of reflection, his unyielding principles, and the legacy he left behind.

As I write these pages, I do so not just as a son, but as a student of his vision. **To my father, to the students he nurtured, and to the generations yet to come, this is your story.**

El Hadj Saad Oumar Toure
A visionary educator and reformer whose impact on Islamic education continues to inspire generations.

Introduction

In the heart of **West Africa**, where the **Niger River** cradles the historic city of **Ségou**, a visionary was born, a man whose dream would challenge traditions, reshape Islamic education, and leave an indelible mark on generations. **El Hadj Saad Oumar Toure** was more than an educator; he was a reformer, a scholar, and a man of unshakable faith.

At a time when **French colonial rule** sought to dominate African education, Saad Oumar found himself caught between two worlds, the deep-rooted **Islamic teachings of his ancestors** and the **French colonial school system** that was forcibly imposed on him. The tension between these two spheres ignited his lifelong mission: to **preserve faith while embracing structured learning**.

In West Africa, French colonial authorities not only imposed **their language and educational system** but also forced **military recruitment** upon families, taking the **firstborn male** of each household to be trained in their schools before drafting them into the colonial military forces. What was meant as a means of control became, for Saad, an opportunity. Observing the **structured nature of their system**, he **adapted and implemented its methodology** to develop an **Islamic educational framework**—one that upheld **Quranic teachings while integrating organization and structure**.

His **big dream** was more than just a vision, it was a calling. Seeing children **struggle to access knowledge**, he realized that education was **the key to**

preserving both faith and progress. In **1946**, with **unwavering determination** and against **fierce opposition**, he founded **Medersah Sébil El Falah**—a groundbreaking institution that blended **traditional Islamic teachings with modern educational tools**.

Yet, this is not just the story of a school. It is the **untold story** of a man who **faced rejection, sacrificed personal comfort, and stood firm in his convictions**. A man whose **work ethic, humility, and love for his people** fueled his fight for something greater than himself. His methods were challenged, his ideas resisted, but through perseverance, he **transformed the landscape of education for generations to come**.

This book delves deep into the **struggles, triumphs, and sacrifices** of **El Hadj Saad Oumar Toure**. Through **his life, his dreams, and his legacy**, we uncover a profound lesson—that **true change requires faith, resilience, and the courage to stand alone until others see the light**.

CHAPTER I:

Early Life and Background

❖ ❖ ❖

Early Childhood & Family Influence

El Hadj Saad Oumar Toure was born in **1911** in **Dougounikoro**, a village near **Ségou, Mali**. His early years unfolded in a deeply spiritual and disciplined household, where **Islamic education, poetry, and Arabic literature** were woven into daily life.

His father, **Oumar Seydou Djelian Toure**, was a **respected poet and Arabic literature teacher**. His mastery of language was not merely an art—it was a means of preserving **faith, history, and identity**.

Through poetry, Oumar honored **Islamic teachings**, crafting verses that resonated throughout the community. It was from his father that young Saad first encountered the **beauty of Arabic expression** and the **depth of Quranic wisdom**.

His mother, **Aba Daou**, was known for her **wisdom, resilience, and nurturing spirit**. She instilled in him **patience, compassion, and hard work**—values that would later define his leadership and educational philosophy. With a father who shaped his **intellectual and linguistic development** and a mother who **cultivated his strength of character**, Saad's upbringing laid the foundation for the visionary leader he would become.

At the age of **seven**, Saad began his **Quranic education**, learning the **Arabic alphabet** and **reciting verses** under his father's guidance. Unlike many children of his time, he displayed an **extraordinary ability** to **memorize and interpret** the Quran. By the age of **nine**, he had already memorized **one-fourth of the Quran**—a remarkable feat that set him apart from his peers.

His evenings were spent in **group study sessions**, where he and **five or six other children** gathered to recite, discuss, and refine their understanding of Islamic teachings. These sessions were more than just lessons; they were a **way of life**. After studying, they **shared meals, reflected on their learning**, and returned home—where Saad would **continue asking questions**, eager to deepen his knowledge.

A Child of Both Strength and Strategy

Beyond his **intellectual pursuits**, young Saad was also **physically active**. He was known as a **remarkably fast runner** and often challenged himself by **jumping over ropes set to his height**, constantly testing his **agility and endurance**.

His **competitive spirit** was evident even in play—he pushed himself to **jump higher, run faster, and master new challenges**. This **determination and discipline**, which made him excel in sports, would later define his character as an **educator and leader**. Just as he sought to push beyond limits in **physical challenges**, he would later **push beyond barriers in** education**, setting **new standards for Islamic learning**.

Curiosity and Intellectual Hunger

As a child, Saad was known for his **relentless pursuit of knowledge**. He **engaged his father, teachers, and elders** in deep conversations, seeking **clarity on complex religious and philosophical matters**. His intellectual hunger and ability to grasp intricate concepts **foreshadowed the educator and reformer he would become**.

These early experiences **not only shaped Saad's faith** but also **planted the seeds of his educational vision**.

- **From his father**, he learned **the power of language and storytelling**.
- **From his mother**, he inherited **compassion, resilience, and perseverance**.
- **From his Quranic studies**, he discovered **the transformative power of knowledge**.

His childhood prepared him for the battles and achievements that lay ahead—**French colonialism, community resistance, and the creation of an educational system that would stand the test of time.**

CHAPTER II:

Education & Overcoming Challenges

By the time **Saad Oumar Toure** reached **twelve years old**, he had already shown **remarkable intelligence** and **deep dedication to Islamic education**. However, the next phase of his life would **test his resilience, faith, and ability to navigate a system imposed on his people**.

Forced into the French Colonial School System

In **1923**, when Saad was barely a teenager, the **French colonial administration** enforced a new policy—**all firstborn males of every household** were to be **forcibly enrolled in French schools**. The colonial government had a clear objective: **to strip native children of their traditional Islamic education and assimilate them into the French system**.

For **Saad's family**, this was **a devastating moment**. His father, **Oumar Seydou Toure**, strongly **opposed French education**, fearing that it would **erode Islamic values**. In their household, the **French language was viewed as a foreign and dangerous influence**—so much so that **French books were forbidden inside their home**.

When **Saad was taken to the French school**, it was **not with his family's blessing** but under **forced enrollment policies**, similar to **military conscription**. His **father never accompanied him, nor did he acknowledge the school** as a **legitimate institution**. In the eyes of his family, **this was not education—it was a test of faith**.

To make matters worse, **Saad's father strictly forbade him from speaking French** or bringing home any books related to the colonial school. If he was ever caught **uttering a word of French** inside the house, he was punished immediately.

One day, while **speaking with a younger sibling at home**, Saad **instinctively responded with the word "oui" (yes) in French**. His father, overhearing him, reacted instantly—Saad was **severely disciplined**. This moment **deeply imprinted in his memory** the painful reality of **balancing respect for his family's values with the unavoidable influence of colonial education**.

Balancing French Education with Islamic Studies

Despite the **strict opposition at home, Saad excelled** in the **French school**. His natural **intelligence and discipline**, honed from years of **Quranic memorization**, helped him quickly grasp subjects like **mathematics, literature, and science**.

However, because he was **not allowed to study French materials at home**, he had to adopt **a unique strategy**:

- **He memorized everything in class** and reviewed lessons mentally.
- **He studied during recess and after school**, when he could still access his books.
- **He asked classmates to help him revise secretly**, avoiding any mention of French at home.

This **secret dual education** made Saad **one of the top students in his French school**, despite being **restricted from studying outside the classroom**. Incredibly, he **completed the six-year primary education cycle in just four years**, a testament to **his brilliance and relentless work ethic**.

Winning His Father's Respect

Saad's **father continued to see French education as a threat**—until one particular moment **changed everything**.

By the **late 1920s**, his father **began receiving official documents and letters from French authorities**, all written in **French**. Unable to read them, he had to **rely on outsiders to translate**, which often left him **vulnerable to misinterpretations and misinformation**.

One evening, **Saad was called into the family sitting room**. His father handed him a crinkled official letter and said,

"Read this for me."

Saad's **heart raced**. He carefully **unfolded the letter** and began reading it aloud in **French**, translating each sentence into **Arabic** so his father could understand. The **room fell silent** as his father, brothers, and uncles listened.

When he finished, his father **looked at him with new eyes**. After **years of resisting**, he finally understood that **French knowledge could be a tool, not a weapon**.

For the first time, **Saad was not just a student—he was the family's translator, their bridge to the** outside world. His father never forbade him from speaking French again.

Overcoming the Colonial Trap

The **French school system** in **West Africa** followed a clear agenda:

1. **Teach students just enough to serve the administration.**
2. **After completing primary school (sixth grade), enlist them into the French colonial military.**

Many young boys like Saad had no choice—after finishing sixth grade, they were often drafted into military service under the French army.
However, in 1930, a major event disrupted French control: **political and economic turmoil weakened the colonial administration.** The colonial authorities, who had planned to recruit Saad and others into their army, were suddenly thrown into a crisis. **This instability delayed their plans, giving Saad an opportunity to escape enlistment.**

Instead of being **forced into the military**, he was allowed to **return home**, where he immediately **refocused on Islamic education**.

Now free from colonial demands, Saad dedicated himself to Arabic studies and the Quran, deepening his knowledge over the next few years.

This period **transformed him**. Instead of **following the path the French had set for him**, he took the **knowledge they had given him** and used it to **strengthen Islamic education** in his region.

His next mission? **Building a new system where Islamic knowledge could flourish without colonial interference**—a dream that would soon become **Medersah Sébil El Falah**.

Navigating Two Worlds: A Personal Awakening

Balancing **French education** with his **Islamic upbringing** was not just a **physical struggle** for **Saad Oumar Toure**—it was a **mental and spiritual** one.

Each day, he would **memorize Quranic verses** and **study Islamic sciences** under his **father's strict guidance**. Then, he would step into the **French classroom**, where he was required to **write, debate, and analyze texts** in a **structured system**.

As he advanced in both worlds, a troubling **question began to form in his mind**:

- **Why could he easily write and express himself in French but struggled to do the same in Arabic?**
- **Why did Quranic education take years of memorization, yet in just four years of French school, he could fluently communicate and compose essays?**

At first, he **feared that the French system was simply superior**, but he soon dismissed that idea—**Islamic scholarship was vast, and Arabic was the language of the Quran**. The issue, he realized, was **not the knowledge itself but the method of teaching it**.

This **realization changed everything**. Instead of **rejecting the French system** as his **father once**

had, Saad saw an **opportunity—what if Islamic education adopted a structured teaching method?**

For the first time, **Saad was not just a student**; he was **an observer, a reformer in the making**.

His **personal analysis** of both systems **planted the seed for his life's work**. He decided that when the **time came**, he would **create a new educational framework**—one that **honored the Quran while implementing modern methods of instruction**.

This vision, though still in its infancy, would later materialize as **Medersah Sébil El Falah**, where Islamic education was **no longer just memorization but an intellectual pursuit**.

A Turning Point: A Merchant with a Mission

After gaining his **father's respect** and **escaping the colonial trap, Saad found himself at a crossroads**. He was young, **intelligent**, and **full of ideas**, yet he was still searching for a way to turn his vision into reality.

Just as he was **beginning to reflect** on his next steps, **his aunt, Zeynab Said Toure, took him under her wing and introduced him to the world of trade**.

At first, **Saad saw this as a detour**, but soon, he realized it was **an opportunity disguised as a challenge**.

CHAPTER III:

The Birth of a Dream: Establishing Medersah Sébil El Falah

By the time **Saad Oumar Toure** turned **35**, his vision had never been clearer. His **life experiences**—navigating **two worlds of education**, enduring **colonial challenges**, mastering **trade**, and translating **knowledge into Arabic**—had all led to **one undeniable realization**:

Islamic education needed a structured system, one that allowed students to grow intellectually while staying rooted in their faith.

With this **mission in his heart, Saad took the boldest step of his life**: he would build an **Islamic school unlike anything that had ever existed in the region**.

A Humble Beginning: The First Classroom

The **very first step** of **Medersah Sébil El Falah** was **modest yet revolutionary**.

Saad **converted a section of his family home** into a classroom, using **his own earnings from trade** to provide students with **table-benches, chalk, and wooden boards**—a stark contrast to the **traditional Quranic schools**, where students **typically sat on mats and wrote on wooden slates**.

His **eldest daughter** became one of the **first students**, sitting proudly in the **front row**, her **small hands clutching her first slate**.

Resistance from the Community

Not everyone welcomed his **new approach**.

- **Local elders and traditional Quran teachers** questioned his methods.
- Some **feared he was introducing Western influences** by incorporating classroom structures **similar to those in the French school**.
- Others **worried** that his reforms might **weaken the purity of Quranic education**.

Rumors spread quickly:

"Why is he using blackboards like the French schools? Is he changing our traditions?"

But **Saad remained unshaken**. He gathered the community, sat them down **just like his students**, and spoke:

"These tools—tables, chairs, and boards—are not here to change your children's faith. They are here to help them learn and understand the Quran better. We are not leaving our traditions; we are strengthening them."

Some **listened and nodded**, while others remained **skeptical**—but **Saad pressed on**.

Winning Support: A Collective Effort

As weeks turned into months, parents began to notice a difference—children at Saad's school were learning faster, reading more fluently, and memorizing with better comprehension.

A turning point came when other Quran teachers saw the results and began to support him. They joined his efforts, helping convince the local government to **certify the transition from traditional Quranic schools to an Islamic educational system (Madrasah).**

In **1948**, after relentless dedication and negotiation, **Saad obtained official authorization from the colonial government to establish Sébil El Falah as a recognized institution.** This moment was a monumental achievement—not only did it legitimize his school in the eyes of the authorities, but it also ensured that Islamic education had a structured and protected place within the region.

This collaboration marked a historic moment—for the first time, Islamic education in the region was **formally recognized beyond traditional methods.** Saad's persistence had turned resistance into acceptance, paving the way for generations of students to receive an education that balanced **faith and structure.**

A Defining Challenge When the School Advanced

As **Sébil El Falah gained more recognition**, Saad **realized that his students needed more than just Quranic education**—they needed **practical knowledge to navigate an evolving world**.

He took a **bold step**:

- **He introduced a French curriculum into the Madrasah—just two hours a week**—not to replace Islamic education, but to **equip students with the tools to thrive while staying rooted in faith.**
- **His approach was revolutionary**, allowing students to **gain a balanced education** without being **forced into full colonial schooling.**

The Colonial Government's Attempt to Buy Him Out

Saad's **reforms** did not go unnoticed. The **French colonial authorities** saw his **growing influence** as a **challenge to their dominance.**

One day, they approached **Saad** with an **offer:**

"We will give you 30 million francs if you agree to transform Sébil El Falah into a fully French school. Quranic education will be reduced to just two hours a week."

The **sum was enormous**—enough to **expand the school** and **secure its future materially.**

But **Saad did not hesitate.** He refused outright, **standing firm in his conviction:**

"Knowledge must serve faith, not replace it. I cannot sell the light we have built here for any price."

The **French authorities were stunned.** They had expected **negotiation,** perhaps a **compromise.** But

Saad's unwavering stance sent a clear message—he would **never trade his mission for money**.

Instead of **breaking him**, their **failed offer solidified his place as a leader in education and faith**. His students, parents, and teachers **rallied behind him, strengthening the school's reputation even further**.

From this moment on, **Sébil El Falah was not just a school**—it was a **symbol of resistance, faith, and progress**.

Early Student Success: Proving the Vision Right

As **Sébil El Falah gained recognition**, its **first wave of students** began to **stand out**—not just in their **Quranic knowledge** but also in their **broader intellectual abilities**.

Saad's **structured approach to Islamic education**, combined with a **limited but purposeful French curriculum**, had a **profound impact**. His students were **more confident, articulate, and well-**

rounded than those from **traditional Quranic schools**.

First Graduated Class of Medersah Sébil El Falah (1959)
El Hadj Saad sits proudly with the first graduating class of Sébil El Falah, marking the beginning of a legacy that would shape Islamic education in West Africa.

A Milestone: The First Graduating Class

In the **first few years**, a **significant milestone** was reached—**the first group of students completed the ninth grade**.

- These students had **mastered Quranic recitation and interpretation**.
- They had a **strong foundation in Arabic grammar, Islamic law, and prophetic traditions**.

- They could **read, write, and communicate in French**, allowing them to **interact in a changing world without compromising their faith**.

"This school is producing scholars who are fluent in Arabic and strong in their faith, yet they can also communicate with the wider world," an elder remarked.

As **Sébil El Falah gained prominence, Saad Oumar Toure sought to expand its impact beyond Ségou**. He envisioned **not just a single institution, but a network of Islamic education centers**, ensuring that knowledge would **reach every corner of the region**.

Thus, the **first batch of graduates** was not just **prepared for further studies**—they were **trained to become educators themselves**.

Among them was **Mohamed Coulibaly**, a **dedicated and gifted student**. Recognizing his **strong leadership** and **deep understanding of Islamic principles**, Saad **designated him to teach for two**

years in a nearby city, as part of the school's **expansion strategy**.

When **Mohamed returned to Sébil El Falah two years later**, he was **no longer just a student**—he was **a teacher**.

His **journey became a model for future graduates**, proving that **Saad's school was not only educating young minds but also producing leaders and educators** who would **spread Islamic knowledge across West Africa**.

This **pioneering approach to Islamic education**—where students were both **learners and future teachers**—solidified **Sébil El Falah's status as a groundbreaking institution**.

A Vision Turning into Reality

For **Saad**, watching **his students succeed** was the **greatest reward**.

He had always **believed that faith and knowledge could coexist**, and **Sébil El Falah** was now the **living proof of that belief.**

Each morning, as he watched his **students arrive at school, carrying their books and walking with pride**, he knew that the **seeds he had planted** were beginning to **flourish.**

CHAPTER IV:

Saad's Personal Contributions: His Books, Innovations, and Growing Influence

With **Sébil El Falah** firmly established, **El Hadj Saad Oumar Toure** expanded his influence **beyond the walls of his school**. His mission was **not confined to a single institution**—his **writings, innovative teaching methods, and fearless commitment to Islamic education** would shape generations.

Revolutionizing Islamic Education Through Innovation

El Hadj Saad sought to **transform Islamic studies** beyond the **traditional memorization-based model**. He introduced:

- **Structured lesson plans** and a **level-based progression** in **Islamic studies**.
- A **curriculum blending Quranic studies, Arabic grammar, and Islamic law** with **logic and history**.
- **Student assessments and evaluations**, a **rare** practice in **Quranic schools** at the time.
- A **French language program (two hours per week)**—not to replace **Islamic education**, but to **equip students for broader opportunities**.

These reforms **challenged the status quo**, sparking **initial resistance**. Yet, **Saad stood firm**, proving that **Islamic education could evolve without losing its essence**.

To **engage the wider community**, he introduced **public preaching events**, where **students recited** and explained **Quranic verses and hadiths** in **town gatherings.** This **innovation** brought Islamic education **beyond the classroom**, reinforcing his vision.

The Scholar & Author: Writing for the Next Generation

Recognizing the **lack of structured learning materials, Saad personally wrote textbooks** to **standardize Islamic education.** His works became **core educational texts** at **Sébil El Falah** and were later **adopted in Islamic schools.**

*El Hadj Saad Oumar Toure's **seminal book on Arabic morphology**, widely taught in schools across Africa, Saudi Arabia, and Morocco. A cornerstone of linguistic education, preserving and enriching **Arabic studies in the world.***

Islamic Theology & Comparative Religion

- **L'Église Actuelle est-elle Chrétienne ou Paulinienne?**
- **Sauvegarder les Élèves Musulmans Contre les Tentatives des Hommes Chrétiens** (A response to **Christian missionary influence**).

Islamic Law & Fiqh

- **Les Perles Précieuses sur le Rite Malékite**
- المبادئ الصرفية(*Morphology of Words*—later adopted in **Saudi Arabia and Morocco**).
- أحكام صوم رمضان(*Rulings on Ramadan Fasting*).

Through these books, **Saad provided structured knowledge**, ensuring that **future generations** had **access to well-organized Islamic education**.

Defying Colonial Influence: A Bold Stand for Islamic Education

As his **influence grew, French colonial authorities** began to **see him as a threat**.

They offered him **30 million francs**—on one condition:

- **Reduce Quranic education to just two hours per week.**
- **Convert the rest of the school into a French-style institution.**

It was a **defining moment. Saad did not hesitate.** He **refused outright**, declaring:

"**Knowledge must serve faith,** not replace it."

His **defiance stunned** the colonial authorities, who were **used to buying compliance.** Despite **political pressure**, Sébil El Falah **continued to thrive**, and **his books gained wider circulation** in **Africa**.

This moment **solidified his reputation**—not just as an **educator**, but as a **defender of Islamic knowledge against colonial erasure**.

A Scholar and a Global Explorer

El Hadj Saad **traveled extensively** in pursuit of **Islamic knowledge** and **educational advancements**.

Departure to Kazakhstan for Islamic Exploration:

El Hadj Saad Oumar Toure (second from the left), leading a delegation from Mali for an Islamic education and research mission in Kazakhstan.

His **journeys included** leading a **research group to Kazakhstan**, where he:

- **Visited Islamic schools**
- **Engaged with scholars**
- **Paid homage at Imam Bukhari's grave**

Beyond religious studies, his **curiosity and broad outlook** led him to **explore diverse fields**: Lenin Museum – Observing **secular education models**, **Textile Industry** – Learning about **economic structures and industrial production.**

These experiences **broadened his perspective**, strengthening his:

- **Dedication to change**
- **Leadership in school management**
- **Faith**

Islamic school visit in Tajikistan

Friday sermon Speech-Biteshcand

Lenin museum

Imam Bukhari Manuscript & Grave

El Hadj Saad's *Pilgrimage to Mecca (1967)*

He also **performed the pilgrimage to Mecca**, a **journey that solidified his spiritual connection** and **earned him the title "El Hadj,"** further **elevating his status** among **scholars and religious leaders**.

Global Recognition & Expanding Influence

El Hadj Saad's **contributions gained international recognition**, securing his place as **one of West Africa's most respected Islamic educators.**

- **His students received scholarships** to **Egypt, Morocco, and Kuwait.**
- **His books became part of the curriculum** around the world.
- **He led research groups** and **engaged with Islamic scholars** across **regions.**

From a **local educator** to a **globally recognized Islamic scholar**, Saad's impact extended far beyond Ségou.

A Legacy in Motion

Through **his books, his teachings, and his firm stand against colonial pressure**, Saad ensured that **Sébil El Falah was not just a school—it was a movement.**

His **journey was far from over**, but the **foundations he laid** would **shape generations to come**.

Medersah Sébil El Falah, Ségou, Mali (Built 1981)
Despite the passage of time, the school remains structurally intact, continuing to serve as a beacon of Islamic education and knowledge.

CHAPTER V:

A Leader Beyond the Classroom: Personal Leadership, Family, and Final Years

El Hadj Saad Oumar Toure was **more than a scholar and educator**—he was a **leader, a mentor, and a father figure** to an entire community. His influence **extended far beyond the classroom**, shaping lives through his **unique leadership style, compassion, and unwavering discipline**.

A Unique Approach to School Management

What **set El Hadj Saad apart** from other school directors was his **exceptional management system**, which focused on **academic excellence, teacher welfare, and community engagement**.

- **Teacher Training & Recognition:** He **organized regular training sessions** and **appreciation events** to ensure teachers were **motivated and continuously improving** their methods.
- **Student Awards & Encouragement:** At the end of **each school year**, the **top three students in every class** were awarded **prizes or school supplies** to encourage **academic excellence and healthy competition**.
- **Teacher Welfare & Support:** He deeply **valued his teachers**, offering:

    - **Family support & financial aid.**
    - **Housing assistance for those in need.**
    - **Early salary payments to ensure stability**, a system even **local French schools had not implemented**.

Through **this holistic approach, students and educators alike thrived**, transforming **Sébil El Falah** into **more than a school—it became a model of leadership and moral guidance**.

Compassion for Students: No Child Left Behind

Although **Sébil El Falah** was a **private Madrasah**, which required **tuition fees, El Hadj Saad refused to let financial hardship** prevent a child from learning.

- If a parent **could not afford tuition**, he would **reduce the fees** or **pay from his own pocket** to ensure the child's education continued.
- He believed **knowledge was a right, not a privilege—education was his moral duty**.

For him, **no child should be deprived of learning** due to poverty.

A Mentor Beyond His Household

Unlike **most parents, Saad took responsibility for all children in the community**.

- If he saw a **child misbehaving in town**, he would **correct them as if they were his own**.
- He believed in **community-based education**—it wasn't just **a parent's role** to discipline a child; it was **a shared responsibility**.
- His school was **an extension of his home**—students weren't just **learners**, they were **his children, his responsibility**.

His mentorship **extended far beyond his family**, shaping the **moral and ethical compass** of his entire community.

Strict but Fair Leadership

El Hadj Saad was **strict, but deeply just**. His **high standards** at school and at home **instilled discipline, respect, and work ethic** in those around him.

- **Academic Excellence:** An **A student** had to **remain an A student**, and a **B student** had to show improvement—or else **face the same discipline as a failing student.**
- **Discipline & Respect:** He was known as **"the guardian of all children in the city"**, ensuring that **whether a child attended his school or not**, they remained **respectful, disciplined, and committed to learning**.

His **firm but fair approach** shaped **generations of students**, instilling in them **hard work, accountability, and a deep sense of moral responsibility**.

CHAPTER VI:

Personal Experience

As a Student

In **1992**, a remarkable milestone was reached for **Sébil Falah** and its students. **Mahamadou Saad Toure**, one of the school's brightest, stepped into the unfamiliar halls of a **full-time French school**, marking the **first time a Sébil Falah graduate** made this leap.

For years, **Sébil Falah** had prepared its students not only with **Quranic knowledge** but also with the **practical skills** needed to succeed in **modern education systems**. That preparation **paid off**, as Mahamadou entered **high school** with confidence.

For **Mahamadou**, the transition was both **thrilling and challenging**.

"I carried my father's teachings with me," he would later say. "**I knew that no matter how different this new environment was, my foundation was strong.**"

The **values of discipline, resilience, and curiosity** instilled at **Sébil Falah** became his **guiding light**.

The news of his success **spread quickly**. Families who had once been **skeptical** of Sébil Falah's **dual approach to education** began to **see its value**.

- **Parents from nearby villages and towns** started enrolling their children, eager to give them the **same opportunities**.
- **Mahamadou's achievement** inspired a **wave of confidence** in the community, proving that **faith and modern education** could **go hand in hand**.

This moment marked the **beginning of a new era** for **Sébil Falah**.

Each year, more **graduates followed in Mahamadou's footsteps,** joining **French high schools** and **excelling in their studies**. The **Madrasah's reputation** grew **not just locally** but **across the region,** solidifying its place as a **pioneer in holistic education.**

For **Sa'ad,** seeing his **students succeed** in both **Islamic and modern education** was the **fulfillment of a lifelong dream.** As he watched **Mahamadou and others rise to new heights,** he knew that **the seeds he had sown** were **blossoming into a legacy that would endure for generations.**

The Contrast Between Father and Son's Experience

My father, **El Hadj Saad,** was **forced to join a French school** under **colonial rule. It was never a choice** for him or his family.

But for me, **a scholarship was available for Egypt.**

One day, he called me and asked:

"Do you want to leave me here and your mother?"

I nodded my head, thinking to myself:

"Oh, maybe there is a scholarship for me to study abroad."

But I was also **his first-hand helper**, and I understood that **his question was not as straightforward as it seemed.**

He was **testing my priorities.**

So instead, I responded:

"Okay, Dad, I want to go to a full-time French school."

Oh my God, **that moment was special**!

He **smiled** and **reminded me** of his own **early life**— how he could **never have even dreamed of mentioning such a thing** to his father.

But for me, **he said yes.**

And that's how **I became the first of his children** to follow that path, **though all 25 of his children studied at his school (Madrasah).**

Final Years: A Life Dedicated Until the Last Breath

Even in his **final years**, El Hadj Saad remained **deeply dedicated** to his school. His **last days** were spent in **deep reflection**, ensuring that **his legacy** would continue.

I was my father's **right hand** for the **last few years** of his life. I remember how many times he had **narrated his own biography** to visitors and to us at home. I felt that he was **leaving behind a message**—a **silent hope** that when the time came, **I would share his story**.

On my **21st birthday**, I woke up to find my father, **El Hadj Saad, bedridden and breathing heavily.** He was **weeping** and feeling **sorrowful** that he had **missed school that day.**

In fact, he had never missed a school-day from the **first day he opened Sébil Falah** to his **final moments**, except when traveling for **Islamic conferences or important meetings**.

That was how **deeply he stood firm** for his **establishment**.

His dedication **was unwavering**. Even as his **school gained international recognition**, he remained **deeply involved**, believing that **his presence was essential**.

His **philosophy of education, discipline, and faith** continues to **inspire generations**.

In **1997**, he passed away, marking **the end of an era**. His **funeral was not just a local event—it was a national and international moment of mourning**. **Scholars, students, and leaders gathered** to honor the man who had **transformed the face of education in West Africa**.

Why This Matters

This is not just **my story**—it is the story of a **man who shaped generations**.

A **father who built a legacy**.

A **leader who refused to compromise his vision**.

A **scholar who proved that knowledge and faith can coexist**.

A **mentor who uplifted his community and family**.

And a **teacher whose light still shines through his students today**.

His journey was not just **his own**—it was a **pathway for those who came after him**. And through **this book**, his **legacy will continue to live on**.

CHAPTER VII:

The Living Legacy of El Hadj Saad Oumar Toure: A Legacy That Transcends Time

❖ ❖ ❖

EL Hadj Saad Oumar Toure was more than an educator—he was a reformer, a leader, and a guardian of knowledge. His dedication to Islamic education and community empowerment did not end with his passing; it continues to shape generations and inspire future leaders.

- His children followed in his footsteps—**13 of them earned scholarships to study in Al-Azhar (Egypt), Tunisia, and Kuwait,** furthering Islamic education.

- His eldest son became the **Assistant Director of UNESCO in Morocco,** continuing his commitment to global education.

- His book "**Morphology of Words**" became a foundational text in **Arabia.**

- His Madrasah, **Sébil El Falah,** remains a beacon of Islamic education, producing **scholars, teachers, and leaders.**

El Hadj Saad's legacy extends far beyond the walls of his Madrasah. His life's work defied colonial pressures, **mentored thousands, and built an institution that still thrives today.** Through his teachings, his books, and the generations he guided, he left behind more than a school—**he left a movement, a vision, and a lesson for the world.**

His story is **not just history—it is a guiding light** for future educators, scholars, and leaders. His unwavering commitment to faith, knowledge, and perseverance remains a **testament to the power of one man's dream to change the world.**

Author's Note

Driven by a deep **passion for storytelling and historical preservation**, I have dedicated myself to ensuring that my father's remarkable contributions to Islamic education in West Africa are recognized and remembered. **His journey was one of resilience, faith, and an unshakable commitment to knowledge**—one that not only shaped a generation but continues to inspire long after his passing.

Through this book, **I sought to bring to light the untold story of a man whose vision defied limitations, whose determination overcame obstacles, and whose legacy remains a guiding force for future scholars and educators**. It is my hope that his story serves as a source of wisdom, strength, and reflection for all who read it.

May his light continue to shine through the knowledge he imparted and the lives he touched.

Personal Reflection:

A Son's Tribute

EL Hadj Saad Oumar Toure was not just **a historic figure or a pioneer of education**—he was **my father, my mentor, and my guiding light**.

Growing up in **his presence**, I saw firsthand **the discipline, love, and sacrifice** that defined him. He was a **man of conviction**, standing firm in his **principles** even when faced with **challenges that would have broken others**.

I remember **the early mornings** when he would **wake before dawn**, reciting Quranic verses softly as he prepared for the day ahead. His presence at the school was **a pillar of strength**—whether he was **teaching,** managing, or simply watching **his students learn**, he made **every moment count.**

Even **in his final years**, when his body began to tire, his **spirit never wavered**. On his deathbed, his **greatest sorrow was missing a day at school**—proof that his **life's purpose** was never separate from **his mission.**

Today, I walk through the **halls of Sébil El Falah**, and I see **his legacy in every classroom, in every student reciting the Quran, in every teacher shaping young minds**. His **dream did not end with him**—it lives on in **every child who learns under the system he built.**

This book is not just a **chronicle of his journey**—it is **a testament to the power of faith, resilience, and an unshakable vision.**

May his **legacy continue to inspire** those who seek to **preserve knowledge, uplift communities, and stand firm in their beliefs, no matter the challenge.**

www.ingramcontent.com/pod-product-compliance
Lightning Source LLC
Chambersburg PA
CBHW042259090526
44582CB00005B/109